Presents

MUSHROOM TALES - Volume 3

How to win a race!

A Mushroom's view of MOTIVATION!

Mushrooms by Connie Robayo

Tales by David Freeman

Mushroom Parent's Page

Thank you for joining us for this latest
Mushroom Tales Adventure, because...

LEARNING to READ is
EXCITING!
SHARING Time & a LAUGH
is GREAT FUN!
Mushroom Tales
Add a verse with a message
That will last when the
lesson is done!

ISBN-13:978-1507837818 ISBN-10:150783781X

We are proud to be invited to

share a special

moment with you and your

YOUNG MUSHROOM READERS.

May we continue to work together,

teaching children everywhere

the importance of the Three L's of

Mushroom Tales:

To **LOVE**, **LAUGH** and **LEARN**!

With Appreciation

Dedicated to Children Everywhere,

As we teach them

TO LOVE

Every day for its blessings,

TO LAUGH

Every day for the fun of it

&

TO LEARN

Every day, something new.

"The Three L's of Mushroom Tales"

David & Connie

www.MushroomTales.com

How to win a race!

A Mushroom's view of MOTIVATION!

Think of LIFE as a race. It's easy to do.

What kind of a race? Well, that's all up to you.

Your race may be running or playing a game.

It can be with friends or alone, it's really the same.

Now, the ONLY way to win a race is first you have to START.

You can go fast as you can, while beginning slow

may be smart.

You can shoot for the top, but first try it down low.

The key word is START.

Now, get up and "GO"!!!

You can race for best runner
or writer.

YOU choose.

As soon as you START,

you really can't lose.

With every new race, you'll learn things about YOU.

The fun part is finding new things you can do.

Yes, racing is FUN
and it's good
for your heart.

In a race

you move forward and

that's the best part.

Trying new things
can really be fun.

Do your best every time.
That's rule number one.

Don't forget to be patient, when
you try something new,

because,

practice makes perfect

and that's rule number two.

When you try,
you're a WINNER.

You can really go far.

From the moment
you start,
you're already a STAR.

So, this is <u>YOUR DAY</u>.

You can run your own race.

Do your BEST every time!

Now, YOU set the pace.

Yes, this is YOUR TIME.
That's the thing
you should know.

Get ready! Have fun!

On your mark! Get set!

GO!

MUSHROOM PARENTS:

Do you have a lesson or two in mind that could use some help

from some Colorful Mushroom Characters and

a special, Fun-To-Say verse?

Leave us your confidential comments by visiting our website:

www.MushroomTales.com.

Don't forget, also, to look for the Free Downloadable

Coloring Pages & Vocabulary Mixers, with every new publication

www.MushroomTales.com

All Mushroom Tales are available in eBook, Print, Audio Books &
Bilingual (English + Spanish) editions.

You'll find them at (you know):

www.MushroomTales.com

There are Mushrooms with Tales, everywhere!!!

FREE MUSHROOM TALES EBOOKS

We hope that you will join our Mushroom Friends to receive and share a free eBook with each new Mushroom Tales publication. Visit us at **www.MushroomTales.com** to join the fun and for more kid friendly activities.

WE LOVE REVIEWS

We sincerely hope that your family and friends enjoy each of our Mushroom Tales. All of our books are published independently and your opinions are very valuable to us. We would love if you could leave a quick review on Amazon.

Just follow this link to our web page (**www.MushroomTales.com**) and click on this book's cover to get to Amazon.com. On Amazon, please scroll to the bottom of the book page, click on the "Write a customer review" button and rate the book and if you have time, leave Amazon a comment.

We appreciate your time and friendship.

David & Connie

52856479R00021

Made in the USA
Lexington, KY
12 June 2016